Waiting for the Mechanic

Stanley Roger Green

SCOTTISH CONTEMPORARY POETS SERIES

SCOTTISH CULTURAL PRESS

First published 1998
by Scottish Cultural Press
Unit 14, Leith Walk Business Centre
130 Leith Walk
Edinburgh EH6 5DT
Tel: 0131 555 5950 • Fax: 0131 555 5018
e-mail: scp@sol.co.uk

British Library Cataloguing in Publication Data
A catalogue for this book is available from the British Library

ISBN: 1 898218 94 3

The publisher acknowledges subsidy from the Scottish Arts Council
towards the publication of this book

THE SCOTTISH ARTS COUNCIL

Printed and bound by
Cromwell Press Ltd, Trowbridge, Wiltshire

Scottish Contemporary Poets Series
(for further details of this series please contact the publishers)

James Aitchison, *Brain Scans;* 1 898218 91 9
Tom Bryan, *North East Passage;* 1 898218 57 9
Gerry Cambridge, *The Shell House;* 1 898218 34 X
Ken Cockburn, *Souvenirs and Homelands;* 1 898218 93 5
Jenni Daiches, *Mediterranean;* 1 898218 35 8
Robert Davidson, *Total Immersion;* 1 898218 95 1
Valerie Gillies, *The Ringing Rock;* 1 898218 36 6
Stanley Roger Green, *Waiting for the Mechanic;* 1 898218 94 3
William Hershaw, *The Cowdenbeath Man;* 1 898218 68 4
Brian Johnstone, *The Lizard Silence;* 1 898218 54 4
Anne MacLeod, *Standing by Thistles;* 1 898218 66 8
Angus Martin, *The Song of the Quern;* 1 898218 92 7
Ken Morrice, *Talking of Michelangelo;* 1 898218 56 0
Siùsaidh NicNèill, *All My Braided Colours;* 1 898218 55 2
Walter Perrie, *From Milady's Wood;* 1 898218 67 6
Maureen Sangster, *Out of the Urn;* 1 898218 65 X
Kenneth C Steven, *The Missing Days;* 1 898218 37 4

Contents

Foreword by Edwin Morgan   v

Sum of the Parts   1
No Return to Eden   2
Blind Alleys   3
How Comforting   4
Political Prisoner   5
Predictions   6
The Sea My Nurse   7
Encounters at Cramond   8
Decline and Fall   9
Waiting for the Mechanic   10
Gap Site   11
Searching for Spring   12
Pentland Charolais   13
The Imbalance of Nature   14
Cormorants and Cardboard Cities   15
Crested Duck   16
The Farms of Carlops   17
The Great Skuas of Noss   18
Lucky Crow   19
Diary Entry   20
Butterfly   21
Mating Calls   22
Schawpark House   23
Pegasus   24
'Vive la différence!'   25
Love v Friendship   26
Mid-life Review   27
Progress Report   28
Reflections While Bathing   29
Youth   30
Know-all   31
The Escapist   32
Linda WS   33
In Memoriam, Malcolm Gilbertson, Architect   34

Ardnamurchan Scenes
   I – Floodtide at Sanna Beag   35
   II – Sanna Beag, Ardnamurchan   36
   III – Chernobyl Spring 1986   37
Master Races   39
Uncommon Clay   40
Where were the angels?   41
Caveat to a Space Alien   42
Was it Worth it, Akhenaten?   44
The Berbers   45
Crocodile   46
Scorpions   47
'The dogs bark, the caravan moves on'   48
Apollonia in Winter, Cyrenaica   50
Postcard from Leros, Greece   51
Manhattan   52
Lady Well, Clackmannan   53
Eheu Scotia!   54
In Rosslyn Glen   55
A Tollcross Romance   56
The Concept of Peace   57
déjà vu   58

Foreword

Those who have read Stanley Roger Green's earlier collections, *A Suburb of Belsen* and *Advice to Travellers,* will look forward to a further volume from a poet who has always gone his own way and is not easily related to the styles and movements of his time. New readers will find a sinewy commentator and philosopher who has a sharp eye for landscape and the animal world and for the examples and parables that lurk there. Amorous heifers, instinct-driven ants, a crested duck shot and eaten – these are vivid presences, as is also the spider's web on the car front in the title poem, where an argument between husband and wife develops into a comparison between spider and poet. More exotic memories play a strong part in 'The Sea My Nurse' (making a deck hammock on a tramp steamer at night on the equator) and 'Apollonia, Cyrenaica' (girls herding goats past ancient ruins in a desert rain shower). In a typically wry comment on present and past, 'No Return to Eden' admits that our 'doom-conditioned nerves need fiercer thrills' than anything provided by a state of innocence; exile from the garden is no threat, since it is only a heritage park now, which could do with a few new serpents to make it interesting. This is a thought-provoking collection which may err at times on the side of the over-explicit but counteracts this with the range of subjects and experiences it illuminates.

Edwin Morgan

Born in pre-war Edinburgh of 75% Scottish parents. I liked the city but wasn't sorry when war sent me to the countryside, for my safety – only to be bombed there by the Luftwaffe. We live in the Irony Age.

I discovered Clackmannanshire, its woods and rivers, the gorges of the Ochils, the panoramas from Ben Lomond to Berwick Law.

Family tradition and wanderlust led me to Leith Nautical College, and a berth as apprentice cadet on a tramp steamer circling the globe. Poetry began to surge up in fountains of juvenilia, which I had the decency to destroy. The sea was in my bones: but getting lost in the Queensland Bush, being stranded in Fiji, and going AWOL in New Zealand, where I worked on a farm, persuaded me *inter alia* that fate had other plans in store. Once more a landlubber, I planted trees in the highlands until the army claimed another victim, and I was sent to rot in the Libyan Desert. This was teasingly known as 'National Service'. There were compensations: the beauty of the Sahara and the *Jebel,* and the classical ruins of Leptis Magna and Cyrene kept us from moping. Likewise being surrounded by hostile Bedouins, armed to the teeth, who were almost as fierce as a mad Dundonian in Benghazi, who ran amok and routed the garrison, armed merely with broken bottles. And in Derna we were buried up to our necks by a sandstorm; in the mountains, marooned for weeks by a blizzard, etc.

But all good things come to an end. I was at length turned loose on society, there to pursue the careers of, in turn, clerk, factory-hand, tramp, navvy, pant-presser and brush-salesman, before winding up as Principal Architect of Midlothian DC, having previously studied the subject at Edinburgh College of Art. Married twice, with two children.

Acknowledgements

Many of the poems in this collection first appeared in the following publications: *The Scotsman, The Scots Magazine, Chapman, New Writing Scotland, The Countryman, Lines Review, Cencrastus, Spectrum, Northwords, Scotia Review, Poetry Now,* etc.

Sum of the Parts

I took a part of my mind for a walk,
the part that yesterday stayed at home,
brooding on quantum mechanics.

Today it acted the joker, hopping about,
questioning the fallen world, like Lucifer
criticising the handiwork of his betters.

    'Why were the Nine Worthies?
    Why create a geometry where circles
    can't be squared or angles trisected?
    Was the fruit of the orange grove
    named after its colour or vice versa?
    If neologists had decreed otherwise,
    might we have discussed the elasticity
    of rainbows, the dialectics of petunias?
    Since Hitler and Mozart were compatriots
    why are we dismayed when the hawk swoops
    on the dove or when the greater cats sink
    smiling teeth in the necks of gazelles,
    who fall daintily on cue like ballerinas?
    And why does each victim unerringly find
    his assassin, every Messiah his betrayer?'

I do not petition Heaven for answers,
which might reply with Socratic arguments;
only for unity and release from the burden
of wandering without charts or compass,
for the most part, in a land without landmarks,
and partly in circles which I cannot square.

No Return to Eden

No delegated angel person dare loiter
On sentry duty at open rusting gates,
The garden now sublunary, a heritage park
Where forbidden fruit is served with cream.

Lacking the bite of burnt fossil fuels,
Amaranthine fragrance would make us gag,
Lotus on nicotined palates would cloy,
The contrived tableaux of panther and fawn
Would suggest the use of sedative darts.

Doom-conditioned nerves need fiercer thrills –
Banner-headlines presaging Armageddon,
Cramping our guts with iron as statesmen
Fulminate from safe debating chambers.
The weird ambivalence that follows détente...

And how might we fill the nights in Eden
When not outstared by telly's Medusoid eye?
Dawn would find us combing the forest
For serpents to whet new perilous appetites.

If a creaking Jehovah should cast us forth
With clumsy thunderbolts of polystyrene,
We would saunter off, quite jauntily,
Wearing exile like a tourist's sombrero.

Blind Alleys

In a mood of disgruntled complacency
Suddenly I fell through apparent reality
To an enhanced perspective of existence
Where the known and unknown intersect,
Where all was in focus, balanced, radiant!

Yet as I basked in that sublime integrity,
The here-and-now intruded, unity vanished
Like a spent rainbow or fakir shinning up
His magic rope, leaving me wrong-footed,
Once more out of step with the Universe.

Desolate I consult a philosopher, who opines,
'Ultimate reality lies beyond the totality
Of sensory perception and cognitive logic,
Hence it is a numinous given, for theologians,
An ignis fatuus for earthbound enquirers.'

I seek enlightenment from a cosmologist:
'Space-time is curved, maybe a twin-helical
Phenomenon expanding between singularities,'
He explains, 'but to paraphrase Heraclitus,
We can't step twice into the same continuum.'

I bump into a particle physicist, who says,
'God is a joker who plays dice all the time,
A placer of banana-skins, forever throwing
Flies in the ointment, spanners in the works.
Why not, unlike particles, stay in one place?'

I meet a Zen Buddhist under a plastic bo tree:
'It's simple, Man. What is, isn't; what isn't, is!
Yet nothing is, for all things are becoming,
And only fools think they aren't dreaming.
The world is everything that is not the case.'

What could I do but applaud such profundities
With a burst of slow one-handed clapping.

How Comforting

How blandly comforting it must be
to coast along with the bourgeoisie,
a correct response for each contingency,
a prepared attitude for any emergency,
and no need to feel or think too much
or care about philosophy and such –
unless it concerns one's personal ends,
a rise in taxes, a cut in dividends.

Their borrowed tastes lack subtlety:
though some know Camembert from Brie,
and others can easily discern
An old Moselle from a young Sauterne,
At Schubert or Mozart piano recitals
they're hardly touched within their vitals,
and during the intervals gossip and chatter
as if great art were a laughing matter.

When floods drown tribes in delta basins,
they sigh and murmur, 'God has His reasons,'
or if they've stopped believing in Him,
they'll sign a cheque on a passing whim
to purchase blankets for the chartered bus,
and think, 'Thank Heaven that it wasn't us!'

If a new siege should start in Leningrad,
they'd sip their gin and say, 'How sad!'
then refreshed by canapés from the fridge,
resume their game of contract bridge.
And if the Apocalypse should come
and fill the sky with signs of doom,
they'd say, 'How tiresome, but even so,
we could finish the rubber before we go.'

Political Prisoner

The chances of acquittal were zero,
His number was up, his goose cooked.
The judge directed the rigged jury
Like a Government whip, declaring
'Everybody is guilty of something,
If he is innocent of this crime
He shall pay for those unacknowledged.'

Yet he was a card up his own sleeve,
For they couldn't imprison his dreams
Nor his capricious gallows' humour;
So the halter that tied him to a wall
Became a triumphant martyr's garland,
His ball-and-chain a child's plaything,
The bread and gruel a sumptuous feast!

They invested him in a straitjacket,
He wore it with aplomb, like a toga.
They encaged his head in an iron mask,
He rejoiced to discover the mouth-slit
Was capacious enough for all to witness
His pitying smile of forgiveness,
His protrusive wiggling tongue!

You would have laughed at their dumb
Frustration as they came to realise
The efforts to prise loose his secrets
Were burying them deeper than before.
But one day the Warden may seem kindly,
Offer him blandishments and privileges –
Now that could be the testing time…

Predictions

Turn them around, avoid anticlimax:
when thunderstorms are forecast
I pack for the beach, taking camera
to snap bluebirds on the wing.

If floods are said to be due
I plan a picnic by the river,
when azure skies are on the cards
I don galoshes, unfurl an umbrella.

If politicos with banana smiles
herald the rosy dawn of Utopia,
I enrol for a survival course
and con up on speleology;

or if omniscient Chancellors
guarantee economic miracles,
I expect serpentine dole queues
and slump into a depression.

Likewise when inspired prophets
(in daily touch with God almighty)
vouchsafe transcendental bliss
if only we abide by their rules.

And if I hear an evangelist
advising immediate repentance
because judgement-day is nigh,
I stroll off whistling, not *dies irae*
but *O what a beautiful morning!*

The Sea My Nurse

Once I knew true peace – as a youth
On a first sea voyage when the stem
Of an old tramp steamer ploughed
A lonely furrow across blue oceans,
From Land's End to far Tasmania.

When the ship's course intersected
The Equator in a dazzle of amethyst,
I made a hammock of twine and sailcloth,
Rigged it trimly amidships between
A bulkhead cleat and a lifeboat davit.

And at night I would lie cocooned,
Eavesdropping on bow-waves kissing
The hull with incessant goodbyes,
While the black crosstrees designed
Brief stencils against ice-bright skies,

Orion swung from masthead to funnel,
The Southern Cross performed trapeze acts
Along the tightrope of the triatic stay,
And I would fall asleep, the sea my nurse,
The swaying world cradled with stars.

Encounters at Cramond

The familiar and strange meet here:
Children at noontide, lovers at dusk,

Meadows rub shoulders with beaches,
Strutting crows hobnob with seagulls,

Curlews in pools yodel to blackbirds.
Swans commune only with reflections

On the river, which sidles towards
Tides that never play hard to get.

Cattle with dewy eyes like film-stars
Ogle the island where dog-paddling seals

Once nosed in search of singing mermaids
Where now shearwaters flirt with sunlight.

Sand-spurting ponies, their manes flying,
Scent the white-horses with hooves of foam,

The grey firth opens her arms to the sea,
The flowing hills rise to clasp the sky –

And it may be apocryphal but locals say,
Here the Romans foresaw their fate...

Decline and Fall

There's nothing special about dying empires,
 as one withers another sprouts elsewhere.
If super-states like dogs must have their day,
 they must like pantheons expect Götterdämerung.

Portents may be ignored when the centre cracks
 and borders crumble – the palace guard bribed,
drunk or asleep, the geese forget to squawk,
 when puzzled vandals stroll past city gates,

the sentries off on another public holiday,
 swarming with the populace to the hippodrome
or Colosseum, to see pageants of unicorns, pygmies
 and Amazons; or gladiators and overfed lions
take care of secular felons; or mock battles are
 fought with actual swords drawing real blood.

By dusk at symposia in exclusive atria,
 the languid scions of enfeebled dynasties,
recall the glories of their inheritance,
 the triumphant campaigns, the sacred destiny.

'Let's have another crack at the Hun!' they cry,
 as stealthy Visigoths gather behind columns,
to lean on spears, thumb axe-blades, and marvel
 at nude dancers whirling to flute and tabor.

'We taught the lesser breeds to obey!' they hear,
 as guests lean on elbows, slurp Falernian wines;
'We showed them who were masters of the world!...'
 There's no birth without actual pain, real blood.

Waiting for the Mechanic

Haar slips over the town like a moist sock,
Deadening everything and our old Ford car,
Its points being cold, needing a boost,
So we phone for a mechanic and wait...

That's when we see the spider's web
On the car front, shining delicately
Like a filigree medallion of silver
Prinked with diamond points of dew.

'When did you last clean the vehicle?'
Puffs my wife in cartoon bubble-breath,
'Give it a rub-over while we're waiting!'

'What!' I cry, giving her the once-over,
'Destroy this marvel of engineering
Which our whimsical climate
Has transformed to a work of art?

'Note how the symmetry leads the eye
To its central logic, while the dew-drops
Act as grace-notes, modifying the formalism.

'Its designer may be observing us
From under the grille at this moment,
And you want me to wreck this masterpiece
Before his very antennae!'

'Excuses for laziness,' she says coldly,
'Spiders are creepy-crawlies, not artists.
They do what they're programmed to do,
Having no choice in the matter.'

'Which artist has?' I retort, and as though
Programmed, jot these lines in the log-book,
While we wait for the mechanic as our points
Grow damp and cold, needing a boost.

Gap Site

As you pass, the break in the terrace
widens, from a slit of random botany
to a chunk of sky with nibbled edges
between cold-shouldering gables,
an unofficial breathing-space.

Nature the anarchist runs riot,
weeds flourish, sorrel, dandelion,
and every summer wild foxglove
bursts into brief glory. Honey bees
amble by, as if visiting friends.

Someday they'll dance to another
rhythm, when a hoarding's shadow
falls across this outlawed patch,
to announce its days are numbered
with the promise of luxury flats.

The City is tidying up loose ends,
planners are rectifying oversights,
the plot is ripe for development:
nature and the sky will be evicted,
like squatters they have no rights.

When scaffolding arrives, that lyrical
thrush will take his songs elsewhere,
and no passer-by will pause to watch
yellow butterflies explore the ragwort
on mossy ruins, of hearths and lintels…

Searching for Spring

This is where I found it last year –
the river in spate, thorned with debris,
clearing up after the tantrums of winter,
a glassy curtain lungeing over the weir:

Well-groomed drakes preening their colours
before dowdy mates, uptilting and paddling
like mad to keep their heads under the water,
pointed rumps protruding like grinning otters:

White clouds dazzling through pines on the hill,
a midwife breeze feeling the pulse of the land,
and a greenfinch bouncing on a leafless bough,
calling to the world, *I'm here! I'm here!*...

Pentland Charolais

Channel Ferry-lagged and blandly comatose,
A mountain to the foothill of the heifer
Who rubs winsome shoulders with him
While he ruminates on strange pastures,
Glooms with fastidious resignation.

The cow flirts with coy Ayrshire bluntness,
Spreads her ears like erotic wings
To French-kiss his, teases the torpid brute
With notions of bovine *entente cordiale.*
The huge revolving jaw pauses, then resumes.

Throwing modesty to clover-scented winds
She manoeuvres to confront his insouciant head
With tail upraised, her trembling legs apart,
Looks round with lambent eyes, croons softly
And waits... If she could, she would weep.

Silken skin ripples on dune-like haunches
As he adjusts his bulk for action, ponderously,
Like a slow volcano making up its mind...
A' demain peut-être, ma chère, he seems to say,
The wretch lumbering off to graze in peace.

The Imbalance of Nature

Gadflies bite whenever they land
on neck or hand without a sound,
and drink my blood till they cannot stand
then stagger drunkenly around.

This balance I've never understood
when on each other we come to dine,
why I turn septic from gadflies' blood
while gadflies all get drunk on mine.

Cormorants and Cardboard Cities

Here comes winter stalking the moors,
Catching urban ramblers on the hop, who
Assume a right to expect Indian summers.

Not so, greylag geese taken by surprise,
Grazing the fields of shorn barley –
They swirl, rise like smoke, veer south...

A hunchback cormorant flops on a rock
In the reservoir, and as if crucified
Spreads out coal-black wings to dry,

Quite impervious to winter's terrors,
Unaware of city night-folk scrabbling
For the makings of a makeshift home.

Cormorants may ignore remote economies
Which impersonally crucify the young,
Who chant in their broken educated sleep,
'If winter comes can death be far behind?'

If I had a wizard's miraculous wand
I would abracadabra magic carpets, and
They could fly to the moon or Minnesota!

But if I had a house with a hundred rooms,
Would I open doors, roll out red carpets,
Say, 'Welcome, friends, make this your home...'

Crested Duck

The canal a slice of sky reflecting itself,
A no-man's-land of light between rival banks
Brandishing ranks of reeds at each other –
Then I dropped the bird at forty yards
As it angled from my sights to a filigree
Of trees against a dusk laced with stars.

The springer found it in a copse; later
A friend plucked its warm plump carcase,
My wife baked it with herbs, new potatoes.
Some corked claret was mulled gently,
We dined late, talked in mellow comfort
As twilight surrendered to firelight.

Almost I forgot how the crested duck,
Still air fluting through under-feathers,
Had arrowed darkly over the molten sky
Till the flash and crack ripped crashing
Across the phoney peace below a hallowe'en moon,
Its turnip-lantern face, like mine, crestfallen.

The Farms of Carlops

Below Pentland hills, between the woods,
the place-names here evoke the moods
and lives of farm folk dead and gone,
whose traits and foibles linger on.

What sad recluse or outcast tilled
the sombre fields of Lonelybield?
What mortal sage or mind tormented
brooded on life at Deepsykehead?

What bright-eyed wench with ogling charm
bewitched the lads at Blinkbonny Farm?
Were lusty viragos in time past seen
to be ruling the roost at Amazondean?

Did orramen clown and clap their brow
at jokes and high jinks on Kitley Knowe?
What bitter affray bequeathed its rage
to the Quarrel Burn's name in a bygone age?

Yet maybe a truce was imposed that day
by the womenfolk on Honey Brae,
and men of the Steele or Cleikeminn
made peace over ale at Habbie's Inn...

Below Pentland hills, between the woods,
the place-names there evoke the moods
and lives of farm folk dead and gone,
whose traits and foibles linger on.

The Great Skuas of Noss

Facing Norway and sudden vertigo,
Ankles are gripped – I am coaxed
Over a dizzying cliff's edge
To pluck some nodding saxifrage,
Like me, to complete a collection
Though of a species rarer than mine.

My whirling sight plunges a hundred
Fathoms, past galleries of puffins,
Guillemots and terns, kittiwakes
Spinning through blue space
To rocks frilled with echoing foam...

The outraged skuas were ranging
Their nesting grounds that day,
Making Nazi Stukas seem like
Amateurs as they zoomed down
From the sun, up from the moor,

Swooping from all the quarters
Of heaven to avenge the theft –
The moor is an endless trap,
Your streaming hair a net for beaks,
As you run wild-eyed, clutching
Saxifrage like a frail talisman...

Lucky Crow

Look at him! That crow never tires
of staring vacantly at scudding clouds
and lifeless hills, those dull horizons.
Like a grotesque newel on a fence stob
or hunched, bedraggled on sagging wires,

He never wearies of the stupid wind,
the domino games he plays with gulls
when harrows wrinkle the same old loam,
the evening swarms to the familiar wood –
routines that never jade his mind.

Except for hoarse cries who would know
his existential crow-ness did not fit
like a glove of black feathers, while we
must animate this glove-puppet of flesh
to ensure that anarchy remains below.

Diary Entry

After our escape and the mad drive south
from the electronic trap of the city,
no drowning victims gazed more desperately
at sudden rescuers than we did then,
at the tranquil sanctuary of Grasmere.

A boat was hired; adroitly negotiating
contentious geese, we trod the catwalk
and embarked for the deserted island
in the heart of the lake at noontide,
myself rowing like a crazed fugitive.

The boat was beached and taking your hand,
we explored the comfortable eerieness,
oblivious of the hell we had postponed,
followed a wraith of rain sparkling
over alders where a blackbird sang.

After a sojourn at the discreet hotel
with its rosy gardens and lily-white beds,
we would return to the familiar conflicts
of our separate worlds, to face accusers
with their legitimate machinations.

Briefly we had left them on the far shore,
like old demons, and tomorrow was an age away.
Gripping the worn gunwhales, you said,
'We must come here again, when it's all over.'
The geese cackled as we stepped ashore…

Butterfly

A spider weaves between my shoes
as I sit watching your flickering
incandescent brilliance, erratically
flirting with compliant flowers.

Your kaleidoscopic hues vanish
as momentarily you alight on one,
your double wings abruptly closing
like scissor-blades, cutting out light.

How you recall my wayward lady, who,
ablaze with the season's fashion,
flutters around town, flaunting
colours which, though fast, are untrue,

For both you and she in provocative
finery are always on the move, leaving
no trails for others to follow
and both guard your secrets well.

I can pursue neither of you into
your shady haunts, and as I await
your return, other spiders gather
in my mind and begin to weave.

Mating Calls

The amorous rook can merely croak –
To human senses a cacophony –
But to his beloved his cries evoke
The charm of a favourite melody.

The corncrake intoning a serenata
Revolts our ears like a rusty gate,
But to his adoring inamorata
The song is sweetly affectionate.

A warthog grubbing up swampy roots
Who sniffs the spoor of his lady-love,
Conveys his ardour with bestial hoots –
To her as beguiling as a turtle dove.

Lord, why should every beast and bird
All so triumphantly confront
The partners whom they have preferred
With rasping shriek or brutish grunt,

While my tender lyrics are sung alone,
Or linger silent on her answer-phone?

Schawpark House

Over by that birchwood where scattered
    golfers meander like lame grasshoppers,
stood the old mansion, a late work of Adam
    (William the father, not Robert the genius).
Once a laird's house, looking down on it all,
    now its carcase rots under a fairway.

As boys we haunted the ruins like small ghosts,
    entered doorways that gaped like wounds,
trod charred beams warily, that ages ago,
    creaked to quadrilles in chandeliered halls,
where ceilings were ragged oblongs of sky;
    crept down to cellars, imagined as dungeons,

jostled up ropes of crisp ivy to besiege
    picturesque courtyard battlements,
made daring leaps across crenellations,
    exulting in our victory – once startling
a cantankerous barn-owl who screeched,
    brandished talons and flew off in the huff!

If rainfall spattered in dusty foliage
    we sought shelter in tumbledown stables
to watch pools form among worn cobbles,
    echoing it seemed with phantom hoofbeats,
jingling harness, the cries of grooms,
    and listen as dusk fell, for we knew not what…

Officialdom razed the ruins, and new hilltops
    leapt into view, a discreet turf was laid
over the mystery. In archives austere designs
    give nothing away, so only the name survives
on the clubhouse fascia – and by a birchwood,
    a half-hidden dovecot where no birds fly.

(A fugitive and his dog escaped from pursuers down a secret tunnel in the
cellars, supposed to lead to a dovecot. Only the dog emerged alive, half-
eaten by rats. *Local legend.*)

23

Pegasus

Monstrous vision of purity
Challenging pellucid heaven
Or the vast tangle of the world
With wings that could not lift a goat
Yet still suspend huge disbelief

Once I lived with an artist's model
And a kitten we named after Pegasus –
Cotton-wool white, ate like a horse
Each morning flew through the air
To crash-land on our mingled hair

The girl became a whore, last seen
In chauffeur-driven limousine
Wearing a leopard-skin coat
And enigmatic smile, both spurious
But truly, I wish her well

The kitten became a neutered cat
Ate less, abandoned his curious
Ambition to be quadrupedal bird,
Acquired the mask of decorum
I did likewise, was that so absurd?

A squandered vision becomes stale myth
When tribal dreams no longer astound
And ageing pinions flex in vain
When ambition drops on all fours
And walks demurely on common ground

'Vive la différence!'

In the frantic stampede
    of the Olympic hundred metres,
The men appear to be
    running towards something;
In the women's event
    they seem to run away from something.

When men faint,
    they're inclined to pitch forward,
Almost as though
    they were falling on someone.
When women faint,
    they tend to land on their backs,
And they lie there,
    supine, as if in anticipation.

Are these phenomena
    mysteriously connected?
Is this the real prize
    that men are hurrying towards,
And the secret cause
    of why women are hurrying away?

For fleeing women
    often look over their shoulders,
As if they felt at their backs
    the hot breath of pursuing men,
And if they should stumble,
    brute nature would overtake them,
Freud interlocking so
    neatly with their centres of gravity.

Love v Friendship

Love is a voracious tyrant,
it demands it all, and wants it now;
but sated, turns aside and falls asleep.

It bursts like a bombshell hitting
a whizz-bang over no-man's-land, and
for a while, lights up the world.

It is a shimmering rainbow
alighting on a dry bush, making
it flower, then fades like a ghost.

Love is a coloratura diva, rattling
chandeliers, bringing down the roof,
then sneaking out by the stage door.

Friendship wants only what the other
can give, which is returned tenfold:
its loyalty is tacit, its faith secure.

It doesn't need bombast or brilliance,
simply enough light to guide it
to the secret places where tap-roots grow.

Nor is it swayed by chromatic displays
or ephemeral blooms, preferring constancy
instead, the perennial, the evergreen.

Friendship is its own music, an intricate
fugue for two voices, in moto perpetuo,
pianissimo, *con amore*.

Mid-life Review

'Place things neatly in your chest of drawers,'
he was told each night when he was young,
'So when you take them out next morning, the day
starts easily, with order and composure.'

Now he rummages in drawers, never finding what
he seeks among the bric-a-brac of his past –
crushed black ties, passé dinner shirts,
embossed invitations to civic banquets
of ineffable tedium; and faintly perfumed
garments, owners unremembered, and gifts
from old affairs he couldn't wear in public;
piles of bankers' statements and tradesmen's
final reminders, silently conspiring his ruin.

Obsolete passports, some endorsed by consuls,
unfinished journals of travels to countries
he will never see again, of immutable deserts
and oceans as changeable as certain women.

Old snapshots of posing people, once friends,
of toothy graduation ceremonies, young gods
on yachts and mountains, their futures well
in hand like their sheet-lines and ski-sticks;
yellowing letters, a few smudged with tears,
the residue of projects begun with buoyancy,
abandoned with nonchalance… The detritus
of an abundantly disordered existence, and
composure a concept of wondrous obscurity.

The day never starts easily now, guidelines
are vague, the correct thing to do or wear
seldom known or available, and he wonders
how his course might have run, if he'd crammed
that boyhood chest of drawers with chaos.

Progress Report

He saw a stupendous moon the other night,
scattering lustre on wind-riven clouds
and racing silver seas: he only thought,
'There goes that dead old satellite.'

At dawn the scene had blurred with rain,
seeping from grey skies on a sullen firth
by a downcast city in a luckless land,
yet depression didn't cloud his brain.

'Maturity at last, I've come of age!'
he supposed, gloating that never more
would whims play roulette on him, moods
trampoline on nerves like apes in a cage;

No more bitching at the chaos of things,
or heckling statesmen at midnight hours
in the debating forum of his noisy skull;
false hopes wouldn't melt like the wings

of Icarus, for the country of his mind
was now terra cognita, precisely mapped
where had been monster-infested voids,
infinitely vast and dark and blind...

No longer would love (that morbid fever)
perturb him – he had an arrow-proof vest
without sleeves on which to wear his heart:
his wilder passions were curbed for ever.

'So I've won through!' was his first surmise,
for he hadn't gone mad or drowned in a glass –
yet ahead, if the way lay clear and straight,
he could see no distant beckoning prize,

but merely a somnolent landscape, dull
and vacant with dwindling perspectives,
where a hobbled nag moped in a pasture,
champing at dockens by a churchyard wall.

Reflections While Bathing

Gales batter the window with salvos,
Brassieres drip in the wash-hand basin.
I yearn for astounding twin rainbows,
Skylarks between them rehearsing duets.

A radio beyond my toes and bath-taps
Emits with smug urbane detachment
An interlude sonnet by Wordsworth,
Like Falstaff, babbling of green fields.

Rainbows and larks fail to materialise,
The Chopin recital resumes and my wife
Appears with a mouthful of clothes-pegs,
On tiptoe she appends a silk negligé.

'D'you remember that tune?' she mumbles,
Her profiled head and raised arms forming
A broken baroque arch with the mirror,
As she hums the theme off-key as usual.

'The Raindrop Prelude, what else!' I say,
As the panes weep and the mirror steams up.
I remember valedictory lines by Alkman,
A neglected Greek, mourning his youth –

'No longer are my limbs able to bear me...
Would I were a keroulos, the sea-purple
Singing bird that over the wave's flower
Flies, having a careless heart...'

Youth

To shelter from a squall of rain
I ducked into an unknown bookshop,
Passing silent browsers thumbing through
The wisdom and dross of sad histories,
The ageing volumes grouped in ranks
Like tired regiments, time expired.

And there, as if waiting for me,
An early book of mine sought my eye,
As if appealing for deliverance
Like a forlorn brat in an orphanage,
Though keeping good company between
Leaves of Grass and *The Waste Land.*

Furtively I turned pages, exhuming
Bitter traces of my past, as though
Uncovering in a family chest old
Photographs of dead relationships,
Stirred yellowed emotions, a redolence
Of faded passions and dog-eared *angst.*

Could this unhappy stranger, this
Anguished fugitive, have been myself?
Both he and his world now seemed
As remote as ancient Ephesus,
And all his agonies less real
Than the ghost of Torquemada.

Like a thief whose nerve has failed,
Or to avoid guilt by association,
I waited till the aisle was clear
Then replaced my youth on the shelf,
Thinking, *Requiescat in pace,* friend,
And hurried gladly into stinging rain!

Know-all

'He's like a walking library,'
said his wife, when we met,
and he peered over half-moon
spectacles, seeming to wonder
if he may have read me before.

Conversation shrank to a monologue
with no interruptions allowed,
as he pulled subjects from his mind
like volumes from laden shelves,
from Abderites to zymurgy, until
I feared the library would never close.

Only when leaving, I read the sign:
For security reasons close circuit
television has been installed
and I was aware of a hidden watcher
examining my every expression,
as if through eye-slits
of a grandee's portrait
in a baleful midnight movie.

And I guessed that concealed
behind his tissue of truths,
his farrago of stale facts,
was a face under siege, ready
to adjust an eyebrow or insert
a frown, so that none may know
his booklore displayed only fiction,
the section for autobiography
lay under the counter.

I suspect when he's out for a walk
he keeps a careful eye on his shadow,
in case it slips away and whispers
secrets to cracks in the pavement.

The Escapist

The chapter ends, the real world intrudes again –
yet bulwarks still plunge in bloodstained seas
and windtorn shrieks of dying men still echo
through the channels of his bifurcated brain.

He sees the exiled hero surveying the wreck
of ship and hopes, his lady lured altarwards
by wealth, and during his tedious daily tasks,
hears her farewell words, the splintering deck!

They have no life, nor even rank as ghosts,
yet the busy town, the newspapers' threats,
have less substance than old printed tales,
statesmen less meaning, for all their boasts.

Linda WS

Linda practices Scottish law,
her chambers lined with vellum tomes:
she deals in writs, excambions
and sassines for her clients' homes.

But when she opines on title deeds
or wayleaves, in her legal lair,
I see a Greek maid walk the fields,
a wreath of amaranth in her hair.

You'll see her wigged, in weighty style,
clutching her sombre graduate's gown,
conferring with learned peers in court
on niceties of law as handed down;

but as I daydream I hear her sing
while halcyon birds all dumbly stare,
I see her clad in a himation
and pluck from a lyre a Sapphic air.

In Memoriam, Malcolm Gilbertson, Architect

Why so often do the best precede us?
I can visualise a curt nor'land shrug
at such a question, the vivid glint
from your remaining unpatched eye,
as a sudden fully-fledged riposte,
ripe with ribald Shetland mockery,
shot from your grinning black beard.

The ruddy cathedral of Saint Magnus
brimmed with varied mourners that day,
Shetlanders, Orcadians, southrons,
all dumb with grief, angry that death
once more had taken the best from us,
and you cannot now shrug that aside;

nor the crawling cars and slow column
of walking bereaved to the grey hill,
to the quiet place where you were laid
above the voe of brindled waters
and lean headlands you loved so well.
What rig of boat are you steering now
and through what strange skerries?

I doubt if I shall ever witness
a scene more sad than on that hill –
gulls keening in the glittering wind,
dark crowd hunched by a filling grave,
the white-faced kin and stricken wife,
your father and son staring downwards
as the wound in the earth was healed.

Ardnamurchan Scenes

I

Floodtide at Sanna Beag

The tide galumphs toward the shore
like a homecoming truant,
and eager to explain its absence,
trips over thresholds of reefs,

shattering and splintering them,
into smithereens, into schools
of killer whales, puffing fountains
of spray from stony blow-holes.

The whales play tag, then leapfrog
as other waves surge in, crashing
over iridescent dorsal fins
and shining humpbacked boulders.

– Here comes a romping buckaroo
showing off to its siblings –
In hurtles an Atlantic comber
to overwhelm their games, and mine,

as one by one, even the bully-boy,
gasp with a sigh of foam, subside
under a last glare from a spent sun,
and so we all depart...

II
Sanna Beag, Ardnamurchan

Chopping logs for the evening fire
I gash my thumbnail and pain
transfigures the Universe...

Flowers on the machair flinch
from the wind's assaults,
their petals blanch with fright.

The tide with snaking forefinger
gouges sand from the underbelly
of lissom marram-tufted dunes.

Battalions of waves besiege
white-plumed reefs and skerries,
certain of ultimate victory.

Black-hooded cumulus clouds
poise to take demoniac aim
and behead the hills of Rum.

The sun like a bright assassin
leaps clear and stabs the sky
repeatedly with golden knives –

It reels, bleeding like Caesar,
and Night, the cool nurse,
arrives with her bandages.

I lay down the axe, and sucking
my finger, saunter indoors
humming a Hebridean air.

III
Chernobyl Spring 1986

Listen, you daffodils over there!
There's no need to raise
those yellow trumpets
in Nature's praise
this Springtime round –
Man has done it this time,
finally and everywhere,
>   in every clime
>   he's infected the air,
>   poisoned the very ground.

And you neighbouring narcissi,
whiter than untrodden snow,
looking from your guileless world
through windows of innocence,
leaves demurely furled:
>   It won't do, you know,
>   it isn't incense
>   that now you blow.

Likewise you frisky lambs
with fleece so pure and curly,
bleating because your dams
have turned cold and surly
shoulders, to graze awhile.
Soon you'll have something
really to bleat about –
there'll be a complete hiatus
long after our feeble shout.
Man has done for us, and I'll
promise you only this,
>   soon before you know it,
>   or even coitional bliss,
>   you'll get your quietus.

The Man of whom I speak
is no shepherd on the hill,
or fisherman hoping to fill
a creel with lobster and crab,
although a candid physician
        with hand on his heart,
        or immigrant Martian,
        couldn't tell them apart.

The person I mean hides
in streaks in the sky, higher
than those mountain peaks
in the far-off Hebrides.
Once he hid in laboratories,
tinkering with the physics
of Nature's construction:
he gave his discoveries
to politicos, who thundered,
'We must defend our great country
        against enemy action!'
        Thus the fuse was lit
        for global destruction.

But you may survive our fears,
all you insects and flowers,
when retaliative powers
ensure our demise is complete:
just you scatter your seeds
of fritillaries and iris-flags,
over the marshes and peaty hags,
and slumber for ten thousand years.
        Then you may awake
        and spread your wings,
        to celebrate and greet
        unthreatened Springs!

Master Races
(Bermuda 1968)

Ocean and humid air tremble in heat
when, below a royal palm I notice them,
a troop of ants in Indian file, trickling
along an agave's leaf as rhythmically
as raindrops or a ticking clock.

They alight where the leaf's steely tip
touches earth, and bunch uncertainly
before linking to the advancing chain,
route-march back to the agave's stem
and resume the futile elliptical trek.

Some cryptic signal was not decoded,
an occult spanner had slipped into
the machine of antkind, not infallible
after all, with no leader to cry *Halt!*
in that endless trudge to nowhere.

How like my own ambiguous migrations;
but I gaped at this putative master race
that waits until we make one false step,
then inherits the earth in our place,
with none to lead them, not even to hell.

The sun glancing from the amphitheatre
of heaven seemed to yawn, like a bored
spectator at a tedious play, as though
the dilemmas of ants and men were akin,
their confused epics only curtain-raisers.

Uncommon Clay

'Dust thou art, unto dust shall return,'
warns the preacher, implying that forces
of nature and the will of God combine
to validate his scriptural sources,

though science probing beneath my skull
reveals that this anthropoidal brain
encloses others not human at all,
our past is not so simple to explain,

for within us all grows a family tree
of personal molecular biology,
with roots that tap the core of things,
buried in unfathomable mystery.

Shadowy within our original genes
are antediluvian memories,
of roaming tundras with bearded herds,
of swaying cephalopods in bubbling seas...

If I could recall those imprints now,
maybe see again fern forests loom
against blood-red dawns as I spread
membranous wings in a cavern's gloom,

or conceal the sun from my chosen prey
as I swoop to kill from a stony shelf...
If I could restore those occult scenes,
would I like Solon then know myself?

But my memory works like a game of chance,
and even recent events are hard to trace,
and no inklings of ancestral forms
emerge from their cerebral hiding place.

Yet I snatch hope from this amnesia
by conjecturing an eventual brain
that might encase and recall the rest,
and know at last the 'meaning' of man.

Where were the angels?
(13 March 1996)

A quiet town, north of Stirling, east of Ben Lomond,
its mellow peace remembered from schooldays,
drowsing in the shadow of an old cathedral,
abruptly the *mise en scène* for carnage, horror.

That morning some person with death in mind
walked unchecked into a local primary school,
fired off his guns at children and teachers
in the gymnasium, and belatedly shot himself.

Police and psychologists compiled reports,
politicians united in loud condemnations,
called for strategies to prevent recurrence;
clergymen attempted to comfort the bereaved.

With what? 'Blind chance' is no consolation,
nor would a fatalist dare defend his creed –
If all is written and preordained, what brute
prepared this agenda, wrote such a script?

Townships in the carse of Forth and Teith
are no Cities of the Plain, Dunblane no Corinth.
Here Jehovah had no cause to punish wickedness,
or if he had, why should the innocent suffer?

And where were the saints, the guardian angels?
Was the Christian God asleep or deaf, is Heaven
bankrupt of mercy with no tears left to spare?
How could the gods have looked the other way?

Caveat to a Space Alien

If I met an Alien, here's what I'd tell him,
(using telepathy) before our fate befell him.

'My glittering friend, I know this world well,
it's a curious mixture of heaven and hell
and surely must be the most beautiful planet,
but that can't be said for all things upon it.
We have moonbeams, orchids and lithe gazelles,
tropic islands, rainbows, Arcadian dells;
we have Shakespeare, Rembrandt, Mozart *et al.,*
we've built Chartres, the Parthenon, the Taj Mahal,
and a myriad wonders too numerous to mention,
for there's no earthly limit to our invention,
we humans being such an ingenious race –
but are you sure you've come to an ideal place?

'Our past was diabolic before history began,
tribe slaughtered tribe, clan butchered clan;
a century ago we stuffed children down flues
and recently we bumped off millions of Jews.
Nothing can slake our inhuman blood-thirst,
as for wars of religion, they are the worst
and cause more destruction, agony and tears –
one of them lasted for thirty years!

'Our vaunted science which imagines it trod
a very few steps behind a secretive God,
now poisons our genes, our bones and our breath,
it has ringed the world in a noose of death;
our genius for devising satanical tricks
is leading us all to the banks of the Styx.
Already we've cluttered the skies with litter
that'll spin through space for ever and ever.

'So you'd better depart before Security Forces
haul you in for questioning, for they've resources
for making you talk – they would *inter alia*
fix electrodes to that weird genitalia
until you sweat blood and see shooting stars!
Now who would do that on Jupiter or Mars?
But before you blast off, may I make a plea,
is there any room on your space-craft for me?
I know of a short-cut through the stratosphere,
for we've made a few holes in the ozone layer.'

Was it Worth it, Akhenaten?

An odd sprig of the Sun-god, that Pharaoh:
pot-bellied, misshapen, prematurely bald.
What induced him to plump for monotheism,
uproot his court and found a desert city,
abandoning the peerless Nefertiti on the way?
She whose discovered beauty later set trends:
ladies' necks were worn longer that year.
Then, his was thought to stick out too far.

What was so at fault with the old gods
who governed heaven and earth, the wheel
of the seasons, of birth, growth and decay?
(Greeks and Romans used practical pantheons,
kow-towed to deities who were all too human,
who caroused and fornicated like themselves.)

Small wonder the priesthood destroyed him,
struck his provenance from the new temples,
taught the vulgar to revile his contrived name.

The heresy would have sunk into the sands,
had not Moses, sniffing rumours in the market,
espoused his cause, dreamed of an exodus,
browbeat the Hebrews into sullen flight
to a land flowing with unchosen races,
who were plagued only by graven images.

Would our world have suffered so much
had Akhenaten remained to mope at Thebes,
fulfilling his mannered but cosmic role,
embracing his fate and heart-stopping queen?

The Berbers

In the amphitheatre of Sabratha
Or the columnar proscenium of Cyrene,
No crowd scenes in classical ages
Rhubarbed behind the cycloramas:
The chorus was precise in its meaning.

Beyond the portals of city states
Dwelt the Berbers, so styled because
Of locutions which to ears attuned
To Greek or Latin resembled only
The harsh babbling of simians,
Wrangling over brutish needs.

Hence by an irony the aboriginals
Of Barbary were dubbed with a name
From which was derived 'barbarian',
Meaning 'foreigner' – in their own land!

Now the Greek and Roman colonies
Are deserted ruins, but for the Berbers'
Goats and sheep foraging for silphium:
Great Carthage is a feast of crumbs
For scavenging archaeologists.

And now when in a modern theatre
Dido and Aeneas or *Troilus and Cressida*
Is staged, crowds off mutter *Rhubarb!*
To reflect the mood of the hoi polloi.

So the name of a red-stalked vegetable
Has sprouted from a pejorative term
Coined by victorious but vanished races
To describe a surviving desert people,
Who never conquered anything but time.

Crocodile

The crocodile can gape for hours,
indifferent to admonishment,
on swampy banks, in humid bowers,
the picture of astonishment.

What is the underlying cause
that makes him so rudely stare at us,
with bulging eyes and open jaws,
so pointedly to bare at us?

Could it be the presumptuous zest
of men in search of Nilotic sources?
A croc enjoying his noon-day rest
would deplore such waste of resources.

Or is it only archaeological man
which excites his incredulity?
To transplant temples from Aswan
might seem monumental futility.

Or maybe it was vainglorious Cheops,
who built a tomb to reach the skies,
that changed his eyes into organ-stops,
divided his face in vast surprise.

But when I consider higher primates,
scheming and killing for power or pelf,
perhaps using religion to justify these,
then I feel inclined to gape myself.

Scorpions
(Libyan Desert)

They make my flesh horripilate:
even large scorpions are not large,
yet I shrink to Lilliputian size
at the sight of them, imagine claws
gripping me fast as the lethal tail
swoops like a bolt of lightning!

The ancients honoured their archetype
by inclusion in the heavenly ecliptic
for the fond to interpret horoscopes –
to avoid a journey, meet a dark stranger
or make fresh plans for Wednesday.
For me this doesn't confer absolution.

Their images adorn antique artefacts,
terracotta kraters and amphorae, mosaic
murals decorate atria and basilicas,
perhaps as reminders of mortality,
O death where is thy sting made visible.
I admire the art, abhor the subject-matter.

In desert nights they sidle into tents,
crawl into boots, invade your very dreams.
Who could feel compunction when a comrade
drops a split tyre over one, pours petrol
inside? Yet awe is felt as the creature
stabs itself to death in a ring of flames...

'The dogs bark, the caravan moves on'

After the campaign a city was decreed
by the priest-king, planned by savants.
Khayam stretched looms, ordered staves,
Kyza-gar the dove-handed, spun his wheel.

Ziggurat and temple wavered upwards;
between floods slaves were garnered,
blistered and wealed, they fell hourly
from the ramps, the work-chants continuing.

Master builders moved like demigods,
instructing the artisans and overseers,
diligent scribes tallied every item,
the sun like the lash rose and fell.

When the city's first-born was senile
on a day of ordinance his bleared sight
beheld the finished glory, dawn's first smile
warming the pyramid's cone of gold.

Saffron-robed priests thronged stylobates,
arms upraised, welcoming *Ra* to the temple.
The chanting intoned till first firelight,
systra and tabor clamoured till dawn...

As silt from the Euphrates adds layers
to the seabed, time smothered the city:
palaces and temples rose and subsided,
the mighty empire foundered and vanished.

Now squatting scholars stir the detritus
of history till a stela or shard is found,
and one cried, 'Here in splendour and glory
stood the court of Nebuchadnezzar!...'

Few cubits remain, though Khayam's tents
are still hired in a land without shade
or shelter from the desert's afreet winds;
Kyza-gar's wheel has not ceased turning.

At academic parties his art hides in corners,
filled with flowers by the Degas print;
the pots are mementoes of triumphant labours,
while another silt layer invisibly falls.

Apollonia in Winter, Cyrenaica

Whiplash rain wheeling across the sea,
the harbour a foramina, the dusty street
speckled, wrinkled, swept bare by winds
shaking palm-fronds, and billowing out
the blue mottled burnouses of Selima and
her giggling sisters, urging a herd of goats
into town with a clamour of copper bells.

'Is cold, the rain, yes?' gasps Selima,
as they huddle under the lee of my wall,
her smile as fleeting as a stormy moon.
Linguistically tongue-tied, perforce
we converse on simple themes, differences
of culture and politics melting like snow.

By the shore a row of Ionic columns
looms starkly against churning skies,
like sentinels too long at their post
or abandoned in a retreat, while below
in a pool between steep walls, ages ago,
Cleopatra once bathed naked by moonlight.

Above the town in aromatic scrubland
crumbles the wreck of a Barbary fort.
Only time besieges the crenellations,
their defenders gone, at one with the race
who built Cyrene – old before Herodotus
stood here, to gaze in wonder as I do now,
at broken terraces glittering emptily
as they cascade to the crescent bay.

The rain, a pale apparition, drifts over
to the hills, and like small blue clouds
Selima and her sisters prepare to depart.
'Säida!' they chorus, herding the scrawny
tinkling goats across the scrub as nightwinds
gutter in the palms like fretful children
and Cyrene fades into darkness and history.

Postcard from Leros, Greece

Dogs bark at midnight, cocks howl till dawn
when see-sawing scooters roar off to work,
ruffling the eucalyptus tree in the platia
where dusty tavernas yawn themselves awake;
a sullen conscript hoists the national flag.

Platanos straddles a hog-backed ridge,
on either side a motley of terraces
cascade to the bays, Lakki, Alinda, Panteli,
where gaudy caiques await abating winds,
sleek yachts linger like window-shoppers.

Above the town a gaunt Byzantine castle
is photogenic but garrisoned, so cameras
aren't welcome, nor in the nearby church
where in gloom mascara'd martyrs squint
through a millennium of wars and incense.

Last year a tourist in the empty chapel
tried to remove a miraculous gold icon;
it fell at his approach, crushing his legs.
The old doors remain open, exhaling incense,
but no one dares to steal anything now –

except for views of the halcyon Dodecanese,
the ridge where jackdaws circle and goats
shake the silence with grace-notes of bells,
the white ferry unzipping the sky-blue bay,
the quayside alive with folk coming and going.

Manhattan

Egypt of the Pharaohs did not collapse
under the vast expense of pyramids
but from a plethora of tally clerks,
one for every ten gatherers of grain.

Here on this extended checker-board
a hundred towering elongations
thrum with a superfluity of scribes,
reflect a future that fails to work.

Already it trembles: as in vanished Ilium
the towers are topless, truncated by smog,
overseers look down from myopic temples
on perspectives of diminishing progress.

Gases jet through cracks in sidewalks
from a subway's infernal regions, rumbling
below demented traffic in insomniac streets,
police cars wail like souls of the damned.

And even the townsfolk seem a little mad.
'If you want some excitement,' they say,
'Open your window, listen to the screams
from Central Park!...' And they laugh.

Here is the endgame of all Western gambits,
peaking too early, like a frantic climber
clawing at crumbling holds of an overhang,
who can neither advance nor return to base.

Upstate a mountain lion flicks a lazy tail,
under his poncho and head-dress of plastic
eagle feathers, an Indian is drunk and waits
with gloomy relish for the fruits of hubris.

Lady Well, Clackmannan

Ages ago a sea-loch flowed here,
those flat meadows were a sea-bed,
and fish could stare at Roman ships
floating cloud-like overhead,

watch Agricola pointing northwards
to urge his truculent legions on,
to pluck fresh leaves for his laurels
from the tree of Caledon.

When our ancestors repulsed them,
sent them stiff-necked in retreat,
helter-skelter down the braes
on their way to Watling Street,

how the locals would jeer and hurl
rocks and abuse at imperial dregs
of pride, the bedraggled eagle's tail
tucked between its legs.

Consider the quandary of Agricola,
his tortuous chronicles to home:
what would posterity say of him,
what would they whisper in Rome?

The purple has been lost for less,
where friends were, foes would gather.
Subtler tactics are needed, he'd say,
or else would blame the weather.

Today it's quite a different tale,
quieter invasions have crossed the river,
and folk on the braes are hardly aware
they might lose the game for ever.

Eheu Scotia!

'Happy the land with no history,'
         thought Montesquieu.
The converse is also persuasive,
         for Scotland has a surfeit
And groans like an overburdened garron.
         There's hardly a page
Without bloodstains, or a castle
         untainted by treachery,
Few housing schemes are not blighted
         by industrial betrayal;
Yet corrupt treaties are venerated
         as if graven on marble.

If only history could be exported
         like oil or whisky,
We could wave goodbye at the quayside
         to those dangerous ghosts,
Ship them abroad, those costume dramas
         of heroes and princes,
Who pose quaintly on biscuit tins
         or in Hollywood fantasies;
Then folk might straighten their backs,
         cringe less, turn deaf ears
To the siren songs of pragmatists
         manipulating the past.

In Rosslyn Glen

This is a place where poems are born.
Drummond of Hawthornden before me
Midwifed plenty, for court life chafed,
Just as official roles can bore me;
So we retreated to this canyon – long,
Tall-wooded, fragrant with loam and herb,
Vibrant with cushat doves and river-song.

Sometimes we would make a pilgrimage
To the bizarre chapel, Drummond or I,
Not to worship God but summon peace,
Listen for chanted echoes in the sky,
Away from murmurous intrigues, the roar
Of cannon-fire or thunderous motorways
With their illusions of progress in store,

And hear at dusk ripe bird-song swell
Over treetops and hunchbacked castle walls,
Watch daylight fade on hills glimmering
Westward to where new history falls,
Rippling as waves to unimaginable times
When other loiterers may sojourn here
And justify their truancy with rhymes.

A Tollcross Romance

When dusk fell over The Meadows
(where drunks fall over the benches)
a swain whispered to his beloved,
'You are the fairest of wenches!'

When dawn bloomed over Polwarth,
the canal shining pink with sludge,
he left her pad with a blithe farewell,
though his girlfriend didn't budge.

'I'll move in soon,' he said that night,
as they munched ethnic take-aways,
but his routine was nicely balanced
and he always contrived delays.

Up Arthur's Seat they scrambled
in a blizzard one afternoon;
against the wind he bellowed,
'We must do this again, dear, soon!'

They ventured to wider horizons,
and over the Pentlands they'd roam,
till her best shoes were in ruins,
and they'd miss the last bus home.

His wife had done some sleuthing
and she tracked them to their nest.
The bitter scenes I'll spare you,
it's not hard to guess the rest.

At the parting of the sweethearts,
there weren't too many kisses.
'It's over, pal. Finito,' she said,
'nou awa' hame tae y'r missus!'

He haunts Polwarth and The Meadows,
avoids pubs and sporting stadia.
If he passes young lovers, he sighs,
'I too have lived in Arcadia...'

The Concept of Peace

If East and West should clash like cymbals,
leaving a smoking void, a gap in time,
extinction without progeny for all life,
we should not feign surprise, knowing
that conflict like grief is ubiquitous,
an unresting ghost in the machine.

Nature instructs my genes to scatter
reckless seed, while convention directs
the libido down narrower paths, setting
passion and orthodoxy at loggerheads:
the heart is confused, and even the brain
is composed of equal but opposing parts.

Thus we are forever in two minds,
the right half despising the other
for austere pragmatic logic, while
the left side jeers at its neighbour's
emotional perplexities and untenable
intuitions, as wayward as giddy bats.

So who am I to point the finger, shake
a fist or wield a club, at this or that
mad idealogue or upstart demagogue,
when I so incompetently mediate
between my own intractable factions,
fail to make peace within myself?

déjà vu

A rutted cart-track to a pine-fringed hill,
cornfields, a stream by a crumbling mill,

and a winged idea flew up from the corn –
I'd travelled that road before I was born!

Hedgerows ablaze with the poppies' flame,
an old pantiled farm with a Gaelic name,

and a voiceless murmur that seemed to say,
In a former time I had passed that way.

Pennoned clouds soaring over the farm,
a startled curlew's cry of alarm,

and as if a breeze had turned back a page,
I remembered that call from another age...

Sometimes on wakeful nights when rain
raps its knuckles on my window pane,

comes a nagging thought like a broken vow,
Who was I then?... Who am I now?...

Or was a glimpse revealed of a time to be
when a future self remembered me?